KJ's Emotional Day

by **Kentrell Martin** and **Kasey Martin**

The Shelly's Adventures Series

To the Reader

Throughout the book, KJ's hands demonstrate how each highlighted word is signed in American Sign Language (ASL). You will find an alphabet chart at the end of the book.

KJ's Emotional Day by Kentrell Martin and Kasey Martin
Also in The Shelly's Adventures Series: *Shelly Goes to a Fiesta* (English and Spanish), *Shelly Goes to the Zoo, Shelly's Outdoor Adventure, Shelly Meets a New Friend, Shelly Goes to the Bank* and *Kasey's First Day of Basketball Practice*.

Copyright © 2021 by Kentrell Martin
All rights reserved. No part of this publication may be reproduced, copied, or stored in a retrieval system, or transmitted in any form or by any means, electronic, mechanical, photocopying, recording, or in any way for any reason, without the written permission of the publisher.

ISBN: 978-1-953768-01-8
Library of Congress Control Number: 2020921767

Published by Shelly's Adventures LLC
Website: www.shellysadventuresllc.com

Printed and bound in the USA

Illustrations by ePublishing eXperts
Book design by Jill Ronsley, Sun Editing & Book Design, suneditwrite.com

Shelly's Adventures LLC was created to provide children and their parents with reading material that teaches American Sign Language. Shelly's Adventures LLC produces materials that make signing fun for kids, parents and teachers.

This is the first fun-filled book in
The Shelly's Adventures collection from KJ.
KJ is Shelly's Deaf baby brother, and he communicates
using American Sign Language (ASL).
KJ's series teaches signs for emotions, objects, food, numbers,
places, people, pets, activities and so much more!

When KJ woke up this morning,

he was

HAPPY.

"Happy"
Smile and move both hands in circles at same time.

When it was time for him to go to daycare,
he became

SAD.

"Sad"
Bring both hands down and make a **sad** face.

When the teacher asked him his name,

he acted

SHY.

"Shy"
Twist your hand against your cheek and act **shy**.

When it was time to go outside,
he was

EXCITED.

"Excited"
Show excitement and move both hands in a circular motion.

After playing for a while,
he got

BORED.

"Bored"
Twist your finger on the side of your nose.

KJ wanted to play on the seesaw,

but he was

SCARED.

"Scared"
With a scared face, move both hands toward each other.

Two little kids laughed at him,
and that made him

MAD.

"Mad"
Make an angry face and make your hand look like a claw.

He ended up sitting on the seat,
even though he was

NERVOUS.

"Nervous"
Shake both hands as if you are nervous.

After riding for a few minutes,
he felt

BRAVE.

"Brave"
Bring your hands up like you are showing strength.

When KJ turned around and saw his mother,
how did he feel?

SURPRISED!

"Surprised"
Move your finger and thumb up and out, and open your eyes wide.

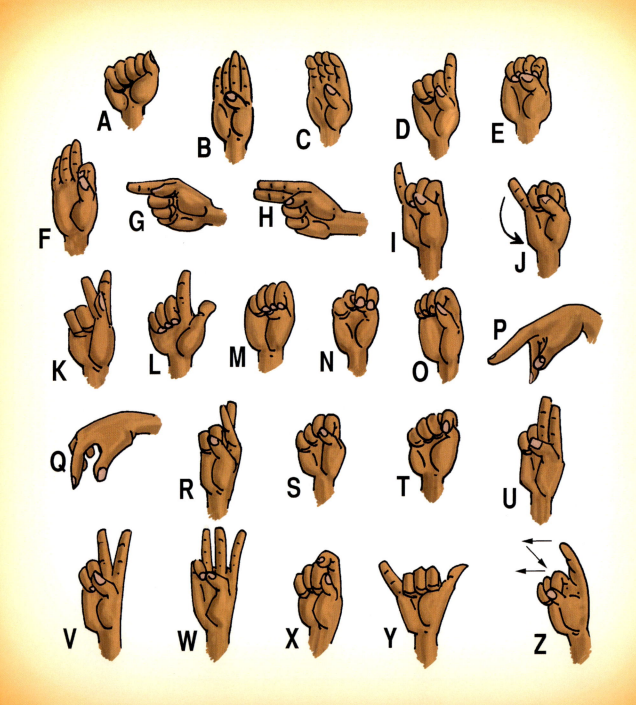

10 Fun Questions about KJ

1. When KJ woke up, how did he feel?

2. When KJ saw his mother, how did he feel?

3. After riding the seesaw, KJ became _____.

4. When it was time to go to daycare, how did KJ feel?

5. KJ ended up sitting on the seat, even though he was _____.

6. When two kids laughed at KJ, how did it make him feel?

7. When the teacher asked KJ his name, he was _____.

8. When it was time to go outside, how did KJ feel?

9. KJ wanted to play on the seesaw, but he was _____.

10. After playing for a while, KJ was _____.

The SHELLY's ADVENTURES Series

CHAPTER BOOKS   PICTURE BOOKS

 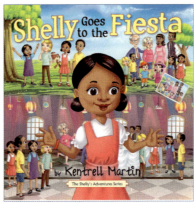 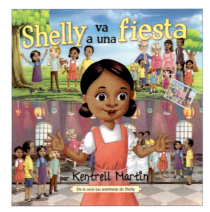

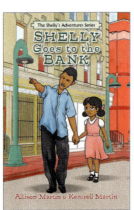 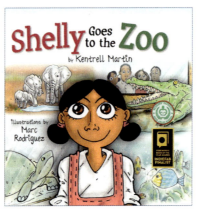 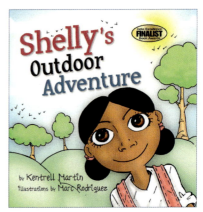

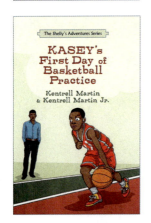

More exciting titles by **Kentrell Martin** coming soon!

Visit Us

Visit our website www.shellysadventures.com to learn more about Shelly's Adventures and to sign up for our mailing list and get the latest deals.

Visit www.shellysadventuresacademy.com to learn more about the Shelly's Adventures ASL Academy.

Visit author Kentrell Martin's Youtube at https://www.youtube.com/user/ShellysAdventuresLLC.

If you'd like to invite Kentrell to your next event please send an email to booking@shellysadventures.com.

If you have a moment, please leave us a review on Amazon to let us know how you liked the book.

Made in the USA
Columbia, SC
21 July 2021